Author
José Sánchez Toledo
j.sancheztoledo@terra.es

Illustrations
Ángel García Pinto

Editorial Manager
Javier Huerta

Published by:
ANDREA PRESS
C/ Talleres, 21 - Pol. Ind. de Alpedrete
28430 Alpedrete (Madrid)
Tel.: 91 857 00 08 - Fax: 91 857 00 48
www.andrea-miniatures.com
andrea@andrea-miniatures.com

Photography
Aisa: 82; Andrea Press: 2, 9, 13, 15, 18, 19, 20, 25, 27, 29b, 29d, 29f, 41, 42, 43, 48, 51, 67, 71, 72, 111, 115, 128, 129, 130, 131, 132, 135; Private collection: 24, 26, 28, 29a, 29,c, 29e, 34, 50, 68, 70, 87, 88a, 88c, 89, 90, 100, 120, 124; Corbis: 8, 14, 19, 20, 21, 40, 56, 57, 58, 76, 77, 78, 86, 88b, 95, 97, 98b, 99, 101, 108, 110, 113b 114, 116, 118, 119, 122, 123; Oronoz: 79, 84, 85, 91, 92, 93, 94, 98a, 109, 112, 113a; Prisma: 11, 36, 73, 74, 117, 133.

Inphographies
Javier Huerta

Layout
Javier Huerta

Printed by
Gráficas Europa S. L. (Spain)

ISBN.: 978-84-96527-89-8
Depósito Legal: S. 985-2008

INDEX

INTRODUCTION
The advent of knighthood

**Crisis in the Roman Empire.
Mobile comitatenses armies**

Throughout the course of history, some events determine the following ones. Thus history is written, the events form a legacy of events, each one an heir to the previous. The study of an epoch cannot be approached without knowledge of the sources that have conditioned this turn of caudal civilization, events and players.

Similarly, after the crisis of the 5th Century, classic Rome learnt the bitter lesson of grandiosity leaving the way open as part of an irresistible cycle for later civilizations, some of which would overshadow their glory and others that would bear witness to spice up the Middle Ages.

The Roman Empire applied the concept of a city-state to the whole Mediterranean basin and an area that extended from the outer reaches of

Northern Britain and Germany to the African sands of the Sahara and what is today Iraq. All those souls lived under a single governmental system, kneeling to the supreme authority of one man. Latin was the common and vehicular language, arbitrating a complex legal system, whose principles are studied to date in law universities in half the world.

The most surprising thing about all this was that the model army comprised of around twenty elite legionary units (with a force of around five thousand men each) assisted by a number of smaller auxiliary units that provided military cover and secured the Empire for about 500 years in the West and for some years more in the East.

Such was the setting in which a new military concept unfolded and the moment arrived when the new recruits to the Roman Army no longer

The ancient splendour of Roman building sunk into widespread neglect and decadence.

came from the heart of the Empire, but rather from the frontiers.

The new generation of militia came from recently Romanised barbaric tribes, especially from 212 A.D. During this year, with the concession of Roman citizenship to all free inhabitants of the Empire, the mentally unbalanced Emperor Caracalla opened the way for that which his father, Septimius Severus, had resisted for so long. Roman cultural idiosyncrasy had been defeated in favour of the barbarisation of the military institution, which had been glorified with its eagles, within the confines of the ancient world and which was one of the fundamental pillars of the success of the Roman Empire.

The new defenders of the City of the Seven Hills retained the term *legion* in some cases, but with less soldiers. Frontier troops, called *limitanei*, were created that, in contrast to the *auxilia* founded by Augusto, only operated locally as a force positioned along the borders. Their participation in combat was rare and they occasionally served as replacements for more important units.

With the continuous breaching of the frontiers, entire tribes paradoxically crossed the frozen Rhine to settle in Roman territory. Instead of expelling them, successive emperors began to adopt the very political custom of authorising their presence and settlement in exchange for signing a treaty, feud, or *foedus*, which made them promise to defend those lands that were theoretically under Roman domination against possible enemy incursions. Thus, the *foederati* were formed, probably one of the most negative points in the disintegration of the classic Roman Army.

The Roman historian Tacitus was one of the first to remark upon the *commitatii*, or personal mounted guards, who accompanied the Germanic warlords. This custom continued throughout the reigns of Diocletian and the Tetrarchs (AD 245–315).

Gallianus was one of the great emperors with a vast force called *comitatus* at his disposal; when assisted by the infantry, these units could reach 30,000 men. Later, in 312, Constantine made great use of this resource in his power struggle against Maxentius, where it won him the victory at the famous Battle of Milvian Bridge. Thus, the mobile or manoeuvre armies were born, also called *comitatenses*. In the High Empire, the safeguard of the frontiers was based on a defensive line of walls or large palisades interspersed with watchtowers and small forts responsible for holding off invasions. These defensive lines, or *limes* were reinforced a short distance away by legionary forces positioned at strategic points.

The barbarisation of the army brought about the introduction of many foreigners, such as these Asian Alans from the steppe.

When the frontiers fell in the Low Empire, the geo-strategic concept changed, imposing a deep, dynamic and flexible defence. Theory stated that the *limitanei* units, on seeing the frontiers attacked should hold their positions and sound the alarm for the mobile armies to beat off the intrusion.

Cavalry prevails over infantry on the battlefield

Ancient armies, both Greek and Roman, gave priority to the infantry as the main element of a battle. For the Egyptians, horses were only useful for drawing chariots that carried the leaders to the front and to carry, what could be called moving platforms of archers. The Classical Greeks used chariots, as the Celts did in their time, to transport their warlords to and from the battlefield. The Scythians, Thracians, Sarmatians and Parthians however, were a useful reference point for the future usage of the horse, without regard to the distances involved. The precursor of cavalry rupture and flanking tactics, as brilliantly outlined by José I. Lago, was Alexander the Great, who transformed his royal guard, or Companions, consisting of some 2100 horsemen, into an authentic shock force. His tactic of 'hammer and anvil' was, however, assisted by an elite contingent of Macedonian phalange infantry equipped with long lances that spread out lineally to form the anvil over which the cavalry moved. Once the enemy was outflanked and surrounded, the whole mounted force acted in a hammer action.

Later, the Roman Armies based their force on the heavy infantry. The great High Imperial Legionary Infantry commanded by Emperor Trajan in the 2nd Century AD, was unstoppable on the battlefield. Together, the individual soldier, due to effective selection, esprit de corps, training and equipment and the Roman military institution with its organisation, discipline and structure, formed an admirable combination. As rightfully highlighted by Arthur Ferrill, the worst thing about the Low Empire was that it substantially diluted the quality of the Roman infantry, favouring instead the mobile armies, the fastest units to react in times of crisis, meaning the cavalry, which became a real elite force. For a detailed study on the Roman Army, consult the book IMPERIUM LEGIONIS by the same author and publisher.

From the 6th Century, a new concept replaced the imperial forces: the Lords of War Armies, mainly composed of *bucellarii*, small private armies equipped and paid for by wealthy, influential people. Although they had been previously employed by great characters, such as Stilicho, these private armies of servants proliferated and provided havens of high security amidst the chaos that characterised the Middle Ages. The relationship between these mounted servants and their lord became the seed to what would happen at the birth of feudalism.

The fast, powerful Hun cavalry pushed from the east a large number of Germanic people that, in turn, produced a real domino effect. After the Battle of Adrianople, the Goth pressure was unstoppable. The main groups were the Visigoths (meaning Goths from the west), the Ostrogoths (Goths from the east), the Alemannii (all men) and the Franks (literally, free men). The latter were to play a dominant role in the proceeding centuries.

A legionary, from the time of Trajan, ready for combat.

Roman soldiers from the Low Empire. Heavy infantry of comitatenses on the right, a limitanei on the left.

books for halting the advance of the Saracen at Poitiers in 732 AD. Of Charles Martel it is said that he carried out a new distribution of territory between his vassal lords, more intelligent and effective than that instigated by the Merovingians, thus laying the foundations for the feudal system. His descendents, Pepin III and his son Charles, later to be known under the sobriquet of 'the Great' or Charlemagne, founded the Carolingian Empire, which determined the fate of Central Europe from 771 to 814 AD.

It was these Carolingian Franks who opened the gates to the Age of Chivalry.

From the Franks emerged the Merovingian Dynasty, a line of kings whose power weakened as their territory became divided between their respective heirs and the Church. The region affected by this system covered an area from present day France to the Netherlands, including some areas of Germany.

Far removed from his Merovingian king was Charles Martel, a bastard from an important family, who became the most powerful man de facto in the kingdom and who ended up fleeing at the end of the 7th Century. After uniting the princedom dominions, he fought against the frisians and Saxons in the Germanic conflicts; Martel won his entry in the history

Cavalry from the late Roman Empire was characterized by its Germanic influence. It can be said that, although Romans were unable to conquer all of Germania with their infantry, they could position their cavalry across the Empire.

THE ARTHURIAN LEGEND

The age of the great migrations

The three or four centuries proceeding the 10th Century are characterised by the continuous migratory fluxes that beset Europe, first from the east and later from the north and south. To the aforementioned movements of Germanic and Asiatic tribes, one must add the Scandinavian peoples who settled in the British Isles and Northern France. From Africa came an unstoppable tide of Muslim people that invaded the Iberian Peninsula and even threatened the eastern enclave of Byzantium. The small Germanic kingdoms of the 6th Century also fell under the sway of Islam, including Suebi, Visigoth and Vandal. In the West, only the Frankish kingdom, already transformed into the Carolingian Empire, strongly resisted the Arabs. The Byzantine Empire did what was required in its own eastern feud, acting as a geo-strategic plug and a base for future operations during the Crusades.

As always in history, we see that consecutive events end up causing an action, or reaction and, thus, it is not strange that the West and the Catholic Church united in reply to the already declared Islamic Holy War with other, equally holy wars, this time called the Crusades.

Continental Europe was profusely affected by the phenomenon of large-scale population movements and the British Isles were no exception in these convulsive times.

In 410 AD, the Roman emperor Honorio, communicated to the inhabitants of Britain by means of a letter his decision to afford no further military support and, in future, they would have to seek their own means of defence. The island's situation would, from that moment, change forever.

Some authors say that it was because of domestic disputes, or the growing need for help from local troops, that the island's inhabitants permitted the Germanics to invade along their coasts in order to use them as auxiliary forces

Sultan Hassan Mosque, Cairo

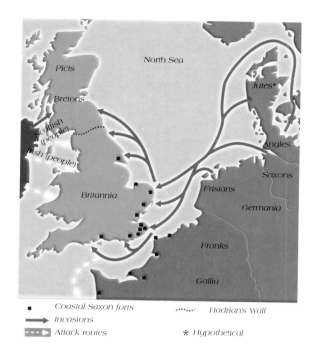

North Sea

Picts

Jutes*

Bretons

Scottish (people)

Angles

Irish (people)

Saxons

Britannia

Frisians

Germania

Franks

Gallia

■   Coastal Saxon forts

→   Invasions

▣▣▶   Attack routes

······   Hadrian's Wall

∗   Hypothetical

against future invasions or to help them with their domestic conflicts. It was yet another example of the earlier mentioned *foederati* that had such an ill-fated influence and long term repercussions.

It was this situation, and the knowledge that Rome had withdrawn forever, that Britain became a goal for all those peoples with excess population, lack of territory or expansionist ideas.

The island received a number of waves, principally Saxons and Angles from the mouth of the Lower Rhine and south of Jutlandia. To them can be added the Scandinavians, such as the people from the north of present day Jutland and the Frisians from what is now the Netherlands. In addition, there was pressure from the Picts from Caledonia (now Scotland) to the North and the Irish from the western neighbouring island.

(Map) Principal invasions suffered by Britannia after the collapse of Roman power.

Soldiers from a comitatenses unit in a historical re-enactment

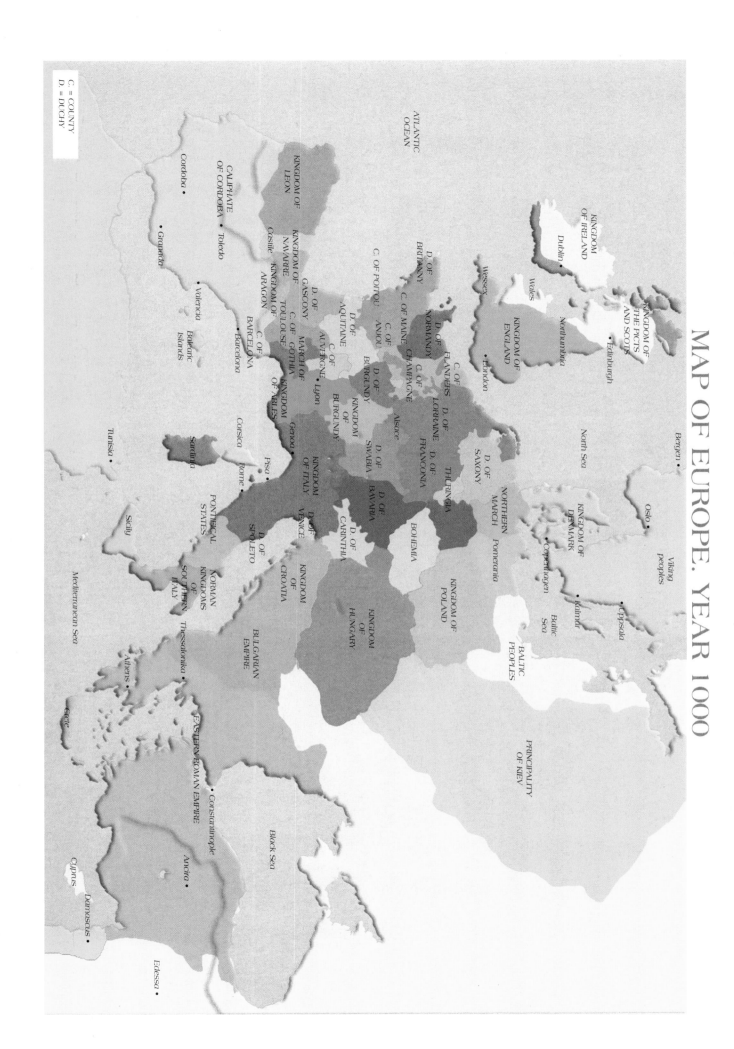

MAP OF EUROPE, YEAR 1000

C. = COUNTY
D. = DUCHY

ATLANTIC OCEAN

KINGDOM OF IRELAND
Dublin •

KINGDOM OF THE PICTS AND SCOTS
Edinburgh •

Wales
Northumbria
Wessex
KINGDOM OF ENGLAND
London •

North Sea

Bergen •

Viking peoples

Oslo •

KINGDOM OF DENMARK
Copenhagen •

Kalmar •
Uppsala •

Baltic Sea

BALTIC PEOPLES

NORTHERN MARCH
Pomerania

KINGDOM OF POLAND

PRINCIPALITY OF KIEV

CALIPHATE OF CORDOBA
Cordoba •
Granada •
Toledo •
Valencia •
Balearic Islands

KINGDOM OF LEON
Castile
KINGDOM OF NAVARRE
KINGDOM OF ARAGON
C. OF BARCELONA
Barcelona •

GASCONY
C. OF GOTHIA
MARCH OF TOULOUSE
D. OF AQUITAINE
C. OF POITOU
D. OF BRITTANY
C. OF MAINE
C. OF ANJOU
C. OF AUVERGNE
Lyon •
D. OF BURGUNDY
KINGDOM OF BURGUNDY
KINGDOM OF ARLES

D. OF NORMANDY
C. OF CHAMPAGNE
C. OF FLANDERS
D. OF LORRAINE
D. OF FRANCONIA
Alsace
D. OF SWABIA
D. OF BAVARIA
D. OF SAXONY
THURINGIA
BOHEMIA
D. OF CARINTHIA

Genoa •
KINGDOM OF ITALY
Pisa •
Corsica
Rome •
Sardinia
Tunisia

PAPAL STATES
D. OF SPOLETO
D. OF VENICE
KINGDOM OF CROATIA
KINGDOM OF HUNGARY

NORMAN KINGDOMS OF SOUTHERN ITALY
Sicily
Mediterranean Sea

BULGARIAN EMPIRE
Thessalonika •
Athens •
Crete

EASTERN ROMAN EMPIRE
Constantinople •
Black Sea
Ancira •
Cyprus
Damascus •
Edessa •

10

The Limes of Britannia and the Real Dux Arthur

During the height of the Roman Empire, Britannia had traditionally configured its boundaries based on two defensive lines, actually situated in Scotland. The first and most well-defended *limes* was the famous Hadrian's Wall, built of dry stone, with forts of various sizes built at intervals. This defensive wall ran approximately from Carlisle to Newcastle-Upon-Tyne and, even today, its remains are still visible. Further north, along the same latitude as Glasgow and Edinburgh, the narrowest part of the island, can be found the most advanced fortified frontier, namely Antonine's Wall, after the emperor who ordered its construction in 138 AD. This dividing boundary was composed of palisades and small wooden forts offering inferior tactical protection and similar to the temporary camp defences used by the Romans. Following Septimius Severus' Empire, this wall was abandoned, returning to Hadrian's Wall as the boundary.

The purpose of the British *limes* were fourfold:

1. To defend the northern frontier, acting as an element of contention against possible invasions or incursions. Thus time and perspective would be gained which would allow the organisation of an effective counter-attack with the appropriate means.

2. To safeguard the Romanisation of the already conquered territory without interference or revolt.

3. To control migrations and tax commerce and the movement of goods in order to conduct censuses and adjust taxes.

4. To establish a secure base for future military operations on enemy territory, from which to provide logistics and cover in the event of forced retreats or unfruitful campaigns.

The final years of imperial domination in Britannia were determined by a government much more military than it was administrative. Hence, the territories were divided into four provinces: *Britannia Prima* to the southwest, with Cirencester as its capital, *Maxima Caesariensis* to the southeast, with London as its capital, *Flavia Caesariensis* in the centre, with present-day Lincoln as its capital and, finally, the northernmost zone where the Hadrian and Antonine Walls were located, with York as the capital, then called *Britannia Secunda*.

These provinces were defended by three military commands, to use the terminology appropriate for the Late Roman Empire. It is thought that the eastern and southern coastal stretches were designated as *Comes Litoris Saxonici*, meaning Saxon Littoral Command. The island's central area appears to have been under the command of a *Comes Britanniarum*, a kind of mobile army command, or *comitatenses* army, like the ones mentioned earlier. However, this *comes* exercised military control over the whole of Britannia, providing support with its mobile army. It is certain that this force was made up of a large contingent of late imperial cavalry. The defence of the violent northern zone, including the walls, fell under the jurisdiction of a *Dux Britanniarum*.

Saxons, Vikings and Normans

The so-called northern peoples assaulted the westernmost part of Europe like an irresistible tide; these races came from Germania and Scandinavia and took by force any area that revealed weakness.

Military leader's helmet found at the Sutton Hoo site and dated between 5th and 7th Centuries AD.

THE DUX
ARTHUR PENDRAGON

According to the legends passed down from generation to generation, the origins of the Arthurian myth date back to the 6ᵗʰ Century and have been collected by a number of authors of medieval romance. Around that time, and because of the continuous power struggles that resulted in the convulsive chaos that overtook Britannia in those dark ages, the figure of the traitor Vortigern, ancient Dux of Britannia, appeared. This perfidious man killed the Dux Britanniarum, thus instigating a conflict with his successor and right-hand man, Ambrosius Aurelius. Vortigern reinforced his position by allowing, or requesting (it is not known which) the support and invasion by the Saxon forces that would be used by Vortigern against the Picts, the Irish and his domestic enemies. The Saxons eventually betrayed Vortigern and he had to take refuge in a remote castle where he found death at the hands of the brothers of the Dux he had killed earlier.

It appears that it is in this context, that Ambrosius Aurelius and Uther Pendragon managed to reunite, under the same standard, the Briton Celts and the descendants of the Romans who once ruled the island. Arthur, Uther's son, became a courageous military leader and, eventually, the new Dux Britanniarum or Dux Bellorum, as he was called later by a 8ᵗʰ Century chronicler, Nennius, the author of the 'Historia Brittonum'. During the 12ᵗʰ Century, Geoffrey of Monmouth recorded Arthur's deeds and described him as a 'King' with the profile and standing of the Middle Age monarchs. During proceeding centuries, Chrétien of Troyes, Thomas Malory, Tennyson and the Victorian and anti-German political interests between the wars and the post-WWII period extolled the myth. In the modern era, Hollywood, the global dream factory, has represented Arthur and his knights as the archetypal heroes reflecting the values of chivalry. However, in recent years, movies have been released that have treated the myth more realistically. Be that as it may, no matter how the figure of Arthur is represented, as a historical warrior or a mythical conglomerate of heroes, he represents the fight of a few brave men against barbarism, defending the values of a civilization of which we are undoubtedly in debt.

Hadrian's Wall
Frontiers became Europe's 'skin' that were continually attacked by external incursions.

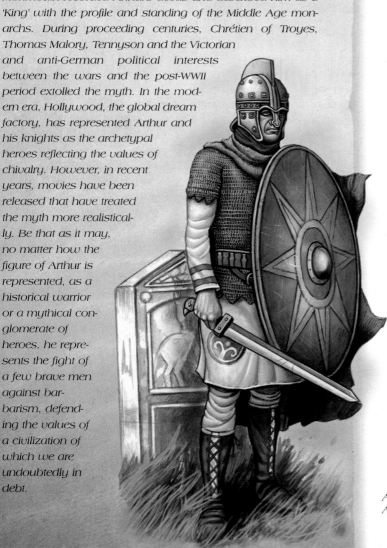

The Saxons, originating from the northern Germanic countries and modern-day Netherlands, together with their blood brothers, the Angles, quickly launched their attack on Britannia. The Saxons, the name originates from the word *seax* meaning long knife, divided the island into four areas: the Saxon kingdom of Essex in the east; Sussex in the south; Wessex in the west; and Middlesex in the centre. In turn, the Angles were responsible for the name *England* from Angleterre. Both peoples controlled Britannia up to the time of the Norman invasion. On the continent, Saxony still remains in modern day Germany, along with various other *Länder*, or federal states of the same ancestral denomination. The Vikings were not a people as such, but rather an ethnic Scandinavian conglomeration of Danes, Norwegians and Swedes.

An artist's rendition of the figure of Dux Arthur as it could have been.

most prosaic of all the elements: sustenance of the body. The plebian serf, in his various manifestations of peasant, shepherd, farmer and artisan, produced the necessary food and materials through sweat and brute force. Thus, the chain of these three medieval states was forged, which sustained European medieval society during those years of transition.

Nevertheless, the desired equilibrium of this natural social order was disturbed by the desire to obtain more land and the never-ending disputes between secular and spiritual powers.

These conflicts would end in serious problems for the sovereigns located at the pinnacle of the feudal pyramid. In its greed for more land, the Church did not hesitate to change the nature of its monastic orders for military functions. Thus, with the excuse of protecting the Holy Lands, the military orders operated with the same tools as the aristocratic knights. Perhaps, the final tragedy of the Templar Order was due to these causes and effects.

The offering of military services was inherent to feudalism; the lord in possession of a castle could, if circumstances so demanded, oblige his vassals to remain inside it as a garrison. Although the serfs usually ran to seek shelter in the castle in the event of danger and, as is logical, the castle offered them protection, there was a figure charged with custody of the castle. Some studies affirm that the exaggerated military pressure suffered by Medieval Europe was responsible for the birth of feudalism. The continuous threat of war was only sustainable with well-connected feudal links that ensured the automatic service of knights highly qualified for the armed profession with their trusty servants armed as infantry or archery pawns. Hence, the mobilisation of a large contingent, capable of confronting any of the many threats that characterised the times, was possible. The elite mounted nobility was the social class that acted as a professional army, permanently mobilised and quickly deployed whenever or wherever the Viking, Arab, Mongol or Magyar incursions so demanded.

The feudal system thus guaranteed the grouping together of a select number of knights around a noble and a castle, which, in turn, provided a certain degree of security at a local level. It is convenient to consider feudalism more as a phenomenon that emerged from the uncertainty of the epoch, in which the power held by the lords guaranteed their subjects at least the safeguarding of their lives and belongings in exchange for their tribute and vassalage. Those who considered themselves too weak to defend themselves were placed under their lord's protection to a greater degree. As such, feudalism was a social reality that responded to the needs of the times. Once again, history can be explained through the causes, circumstances and consequences of the moment.

Re-enactor dressed as a 'Man at arms', belonging to the elite infantry unit.

THE CHIVALRIC IDEAL
Epic poems

Warriors with Principles

One of the most manipulated and misquoted concepts in the history of humanity is that of 'knight'. It arose at a point in history in which the personal attribution of the term led to the presumption that the person in question possessed a series of ethical values and lived by given rules of conduct, a warrior code, and possessed armour and horses.

At a time when the priests-men were dedicated to prayer and spiritual meditation, the peasants-men worked to feed all the hungry mouths and the monarchs-men governed their destinies, another class of men was required to face the dangers of violence and war, two absolute realities that dominated those bloodthirsty times. Furthermore, it was appropriate to instil in this fighting caste the principles of protecting the weakest groups of society from potential abuses of power and injustices derived from the misuse of force. Thus, the ancient ideals of classic Greek philosophers were revived. Under these, the guardians of the state should be loyal, strong, temperate, compassionate with their fellow citizens and ruthless with the enemy. Their power was thus limited to the role of mere protectors.

Modern reconstruction of a medieval knight, 14th or 15th Century

THE HUMAN FACTOR
The knights

Social origin

As the old proverb says, *'not all nobles are knights, but all knights must be nobles'*. Normally, aspiring knights came from the land-holding nobility, with several previous generations of knightly lineage. A knight who was not born a knight had to be invested with the title in a special ceremony that will be outlined later. Originally, it could be said that the knights were an elite force (among the best and most power-ful) created by Charlemagne, the great promoter of feudalism, in order to be able to rely on a highly qualified, equipped and trained cavalry.

The feudal system developed and, over time, when titles and land began to be allocated among the finest, these noble knights took possession of feuds and, in turn, engaged other knights for their personal defence and the protection of their castle and estates. The chain continued, such that one of these knights could be named, by right of his nobility, as lord of a vil-

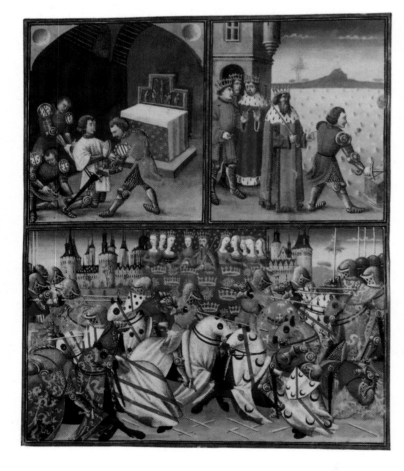

lage around which he owned a territory or estate and, of course, new knights in his service. A new social class of small land-holding knights was created, which maintained a two-way relationship as vassal to some and lord over others. This equestrian order had to be wealthy enough to maintain arms, plate armour, horses and squires, although this premise was sometimes barely achieved. These rural nobles rarely abandoned their possessions in the countryside and when they did, it was always in order to serve his lord or for a social or family commitment. Some, without fortune, but with noble lineage preferred to seek adventure at the tournaments or Crusades, thus obtaining the glory and riches they believed they deserved.

As previously stated, the future knights had their social origins mostly within the rural land-holding nobility. During the 14th and 15th Centuries, a curious phenomenon occurred, as young merchants and

Scene from a medieval book about the life of Galahad, Lancelot's son. He is being knighted in a chapel. King Arthur, Queen Guinevere and Lancelot are also present.

craftsmen entered into knighthood from the high bourgeoisie classes from the flourishing metropolises. This new and thriving nobility from the cities fitted intrinsically with the social, economic, political and military changes that characterised the Early Middle Ages.

Simultaneously, the reverse of this process occurred, as those young men, whose family had been forged by knights of blood lineage for many generations, no longer wished to belong to the same establishment. Similarly, this implied being in the service of their lord, and having to participate in whatever military adventure that he wished to engage in, thereby running the physical and material risks involved and leaving unattended his estates and work-

related affairs for the cause in question. This class of rural knights soon created an economic crisis, necessitating the formation of laws in some countries that obliged nobles in possession of a certain level of wealth to become knights under the threat of reprisal if they refused.

Simultaneously, it became more and more common to arm as knights, simple professional soldiers who had demonstrated an exceptional deed on the battlefield. With the passage of time, the old values were perverted and the glorious old Order of Knighthood degenerated.

Process of Becoming a Knight

Once the noble origins of the candidate had been verified, it was assumed that he had received instruction in the basic concepts of manners and behaviour. It was believed that contact with ladies and other nobles would have made him courteous, clean, pleasant and always servile. With his family, he would have learned to read and write and understand the sacred texts of the Christian faith, as well as other basic skills, including equestrianism, hunting and the use of weapons.

The future knight began his training at the age of ten. He was usually sent to serve as a page in the feudal lord's castle, or that of a superior noble in the family. There he had to take care of himself and take advantage of the occasion to make influential friends. As one of his obligations as page, he served at table the various dignities who visited the castle, hence the young boy humbly learnt the principles of

A medieval illustration from 1450, showing the way a squire had to supply a knight with arms.

WEAPONS AND ARMOUR
Technology in the service of God

Medieval Metallurgy

The knowledge of manufacturing and the handling techniques of metal goes back to the Iron Age during which both Hallstatt's Celtic culture (8th Century B.C.) and the La Téne period were responsible for the arrival of basic metallurgical principals into Europe. During the Roman era, some progress was made in the introduction of steel, especially in Celtic-Iberian swords.

In Scandinavia, during the 8th Century A.D., the Vikings developed a forge, by means of which an iron bar was introduced into a piece of steel in the form of a 'V', which later became amalgamated with the rest of the material. Once this had been achieved, a mixed piece was bent and hammered to obtain a join by soldering the com-

position. Carbon was then added to provide the alloy with greater elasticity and hardness. This was achieved by passing the piece through a coal fire that, by absorption, built up a fine external layer of extraordinary resistance. This process was called 'carbonisation' and gave the edges of the blade and the tip a greater hardness, evidenced by a lighter colour to the blade's core that conserved a greater proportion of iron, was more ductile and flexible. Some surviving blades from the time still retain the armourer's name inscribed, like the one where *Ingelri* can be read. The name of another armourer, *Ulfberht*, is visible on another blade. This is from the Rhine region, near Solingen, Germany, where the metallurgic tradition survives to this day.

Medieval blacksmith during an historical recreation of the Battle of Hastings, 1066.

Over time, the manufacture of steel developed and plate armour and swords were made that were as good as, or even better than those manufactured previously with the soldering and hammered carbonisation technique. Using these processes, steel containing a carbon proportion as high as 2% could be obtained. The technique for forging a top quality sword blade could take up to a whole month and required a large quantity of coal to create and maintain the high temperatures during the long forging process.

In a caved, brick-based furnace with adequate ventilation, a number of layers were laid: first a layer of coke, then one of vegetable coal, iron filings, more coal and then more residue from the burning of mineral coal, known as coke. This was then covered with mud making a fireplace and then lit under the first layer of coke. This forging process lasted several weeks, during which the combustion minerals had to be replaced and constant high temperatures had to be maintained. When it melted, the incandescent iron amalgamated with the carbon derived from the combustion of the various coal components. Thus, an homogenous top quality steel was obtained. Next, came the process of hammering the red-hot steel to remove any foundry bubbles remaining in the metal. Once the piece had been beaten out to twice the length of a normal sword, it was folded to obtain the desired size. These two layers were then compacted and folded again and the process repeated until there were 32 layers for a single piece. This resulted in a steel of both amazing hardness and elasticity. The edges and tip that did not require torsional resistance, but did need to be hard, were forged separately and soldered to the red-hot sword. The blade was alternately repeatedly hammered when red-hot and then plunge cooled with water. Thus, both cohesion and forging were achieved. Finally, the sword was polished and sharpened, and the knight received a weapon manufactured by the most advanced metallurgic technology.

Normans wearing the hauberk and conical helmet with nasal bar.

Defensive Equipment

When analysing the medieval knight's defensive equipment, it is useful to review the type of weapons and assaults the armour had been designed to defend against. The most significant dangers faced by a knight, logically these varied over time and according to the setting and, of course, according to the opponent at the time. The development of armour during the Middle Ages will be explained later; for the moment the more characteristic elements will be reviewed.

HELMETS

The helmets underwent progressive improvements, with a more complete and integral protection at each phase. From the typical conical bascinet, to which a nasal bar was later added, followed by a facemask and then a visor that could be raised, resulting in the great robust closed helmets shaped like a barrel. The advantage of the latter was that they fitted under pressure with the arming coif so that, in the event of strike, the blow could not directly reach the head and, furthermore, the force of the impact was borne by the shoulders. In addition, it protected the neck and, with some models, even the throat. Later, at the beginning of the 15th Century, various designs flourished, among which the Italian *barbuta* and the Gothic knight's *sallet* stand out.

AVENTAIL OR MAIL COIF

The aventail, or mail coif was basically a chain mail hood, sometimes double weave, that also covered the neck. These sometimes incorporated a type of medical mask, also made of chain mail called ventail that was attached to the aventail by means of leather straps.

ARMING COIF

This was a padded protection in the shape of a leather cup with a type of stuffed ring around the top to fix it to the large closed helmets. This should not be confused with the fabric coif, which directly covered the head and over which a leather or light metal bascinet was placed when the conical helmet was worn. The arming coifs were filled with wool, straw or cotton. The arming coif was worn underneath or over the aventail.

HACKETON OR GAMBESSON
AND QUILTED JUPON

The hacketon, aketon or gambesson was a cushioned item like a quilted jacket used since Norman times, worn under the chain mail to absorb the tremendous impact to the body generated by a blow or thrust that the web of the mail coat had managed to stop in the first instance.

As anti-trauma protection, it prevented serious contusions, wounds and bone fractures that could certainly be inflicted by a strike from a good sword, axe or lance. Their origins were probably either Arab or oriental, adopted by the late Franks and Normans, as the word aketon originates from the Arab word *al-qutn*, meaning cotton, one of the materials used for the filling, together with linen and straw. Their use was generalised in the 13th Century. Without armour

Evolution of the helmet.
10th – 15th Centuries.

Following page. Top
Steps to protect the knight's head.
A – Fabric coif. B – Leather or metal bascinet. C – Aventail or mail coif.
D - Mail coif with closed ventail. E - Conical helmet with nasal bar.
F – Mail coif over the aventail. G – Great closed-helmet.

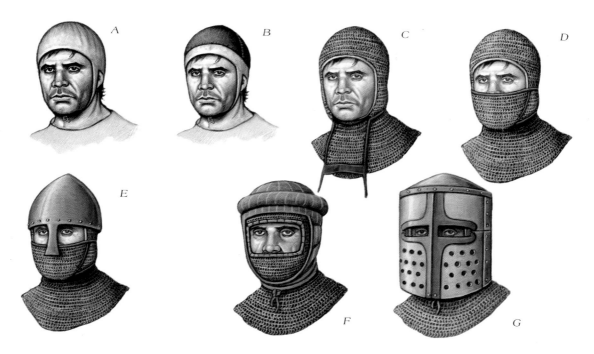

over them, they were worn during training or by men-at-arms and squires who might have lacked the financial resources for a cuirass. If this was the case, they were usually profusely decorated and even reinforced on the exterior.

During the period when full armour was worn (14th and 15th Centuries), the so-called quilted jupon was developed, which reached the hips

and occasionally had chain mail parts and laces to support the metal parts of the armour.

BRIGANDINE

As a means of light protection when travelling through enemy territory, the brigandine was developed in the 14th and 15th Centuries. It consisted of a hard canvas waistcoat with fine metal

The first three figures show the evolution of the mail coat.
The two figures on the right are wearing a brigandine and a quilted jupon respectively.

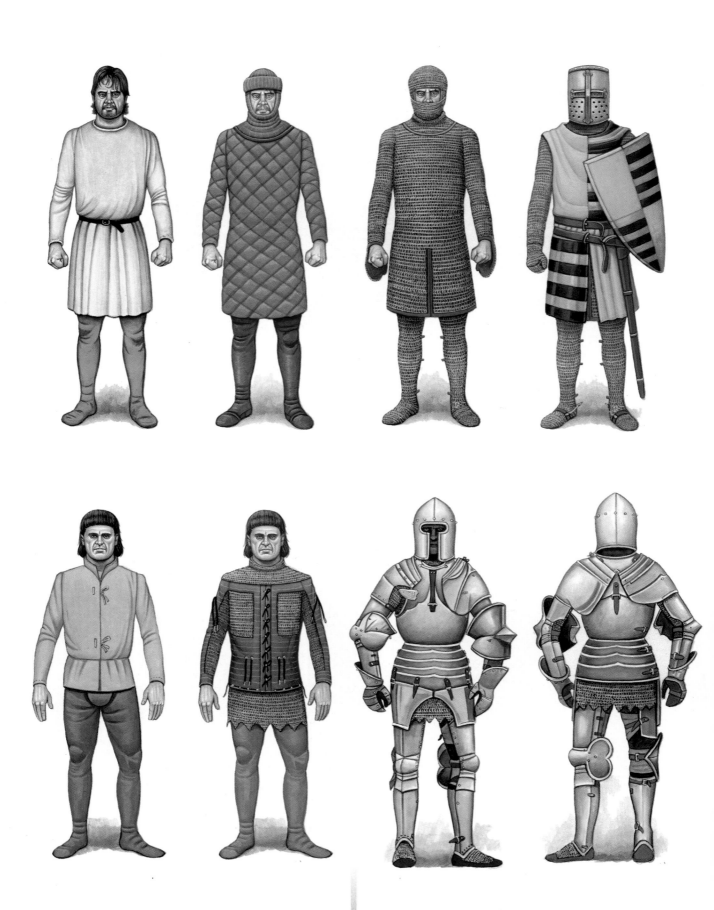

Above: 13th Century knight.

Below: 15th Century knight.

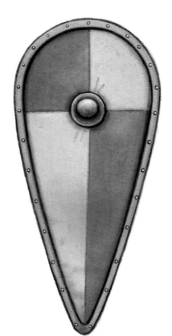

pieces superimposed on the inside and attached by means of a series of clinchs that covered the whole item. They occasionally included chest reinforcements or had short sleeves, and the exterior was usually finished with stout leather.

MAIL SHIRT OR HAUBERK

Mail shirt was the most popular item of armour throughout the whole of the medieval period. Various models existed: chain mail shirt with short sleeves; long shirt reaching the knees known as the hauberk; and a complete chain mail suit with long sleeves and mittens for the hands, chausses for the legs and chain mail sabatons for the feet. When complete metal plate armour began to be used, the custom of wearing a short chain mail shirt (haubergeon) over the padded jupon became popular among knights, to protect those parts not covered by the armour. Sometimes, this jupon was a mixture of padding and chain mail.

PROTECTIVE PLATES AND ARMOUR

As possible threats to the knight (crossbow and longbow) developed, the development of armour also advanced, in an unstoppable arms race of offense and defense: Simple chain mail was replaced by double woven chain mail, then metal plates were added to the arms, legs and breast until, finally, full suits of armour or white armour were created, where the knight was totally covered in metal. The panoplies became more and more complex, especially from the onset of the One Hundred Years War, when the use of the English longbow necessitated the adoption of more efficient countermeasures. The evolution of the medieval knight's body armour will be examined in more detail later.

SHIELDS AND PAVIS

In contrast to the evolution of armour, shields became smaller and smaller over time, as the knight became increasingly covered and protected with metal. This has a logical explanation, as the first kite-shaped shields fulfilled the obvious function of defending the leg exposed to the enemy (usually the left one). As the leg(s) became protected with chain mail and, later,

Evolution of the shield, 10th – 15th Centuries.

with steel cuisees, poleyns and greaves, the long shield was no longer necessary.

The shield became smaller and eventually adopted the shape commonly used as the basis for heraldic crests, called the heater shield, it had the shape of a modern-day ironing board. This developed because it was light, thus allowing it to be easily slung over the shoulder when galloping, supported by a guige, a strap that passed diagonally over the shoulder and opposite hip, so that it could be transported, leaving the left arm free. With full armour and a more developed method of fencing with the bastard sword (hand-and-a-half sword) and the large sword (two handed or spadone), the sword blow was parried with the flat part of the sword. Thus, the shield became less useful and tiresome to carry.

There was also another type of small plate shield, the buckler, that was used both to parry blows and as a weapon. This was used extensively from the 15th Century onwards especially by men not wearing complete armour.

Yet another design was the pavis, a large rectangular shield with a groove on the inside that could be used to support a stake that was fixed

to the ground. With the stake in place, it could be used as a parapet primarily by crossbowmen but also, occasionally, by longbowmen.

Weaponry

SWORD
The sword was, without doubt, the medieval knight's most important and charismatic weapon. This was not only because of the symbolism represented by a weapon in the form of a cross during the time of the Crusades, but also because it was the quintessential weapon that the newly knight received and with which he was invested on the shoulder.

The initial designs were based on a Germanic trunk, (hence we refer to a sword's family tree), which were then amalgamated with ancient Roman and Celtic swords. The 11th Century Norman sword has been defined as the 'mother' of the medieval sword, all later developments being derived from the same design.

Around the year 1000, Western European swords followed the Frankish model, a variation of the Celtic-Roman or the Viking, a design more

*Infantry equipped with lances and swords.
Hastings, 2006*

Horse's bit at idle (A) and in use (B).

means of a halter. Finally, with the horse accoutred with armour and protective skirts, it became difficult to spur it forward in the conventional way. So, longer spurs were introduced in the form of stars that could be felt by the horse through the protective skirt.

HORSE WITH TRAPPINGS AND BARDS. 13TH CENTURY

The knights' horses were also equipped with means of defense, called bards, that were, initially, simple padding like the knights' gambessons. Later, bards were made from leather and, finally, from chain mail. In practice, they consisted of two parts: one that covered the head, neck, breast and forequarters, and another, rear part, which protected the animals' hindquarters. The skirt or trappings, complete with the particular knight's heraldic bearings,

was placed over the bards, and also consisted of front and rear parts.

Beneath the bards, a leather or canvas protection was added to prevent abrasion from the mail coats when galloping. A hard leather, or metal shaffron was usually placed over the head, either instead of the chain mail or over it.

The horse in the illustration wears the typical saddle with high curved pommels that fitted into the back of the hip, and a hard front to protect the

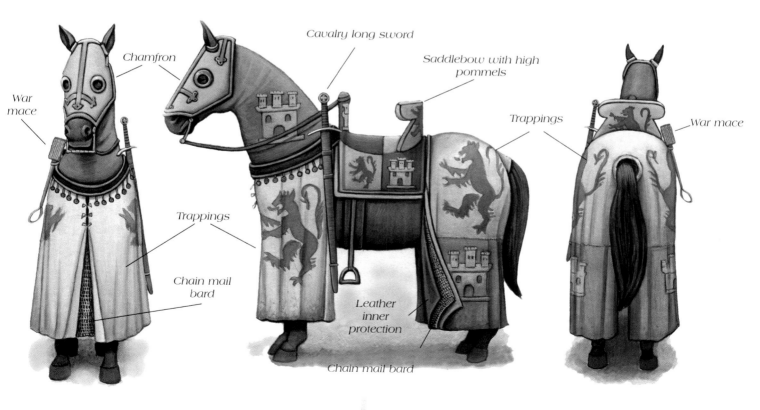

Views of a horse with trappings and chain mail.

knight's genitalia. The long stirrups can also be seen, and a large broadsword for mounted combat. A mace hangs from the other side of the saddle, although this could, of course, have been a battleaxe.

HORSE WITH STEEL ARMOUR
15TH CENTURY

The horse shown here wears a full set of steel plate armour as worn during the 15th and 16th Centuries. It is equipped with a typical harness as used as by Gothic German Knights, and was immensely popular among the nobility and kings of contemporary Europe.

The inside of the plates were covered with a hard leather or padded lining, to protect the horse against rubbing, that were attached to the body by means of large straps. In some specific areas, particularly at the widest part of the horse, such as the breast, the plates were joined and articulated between each other by hinges, thus allowing the horse greater mobility.

As can be seen, the animal wears a chanfron, or shaffron, to protect the forehead with a horn, to make it appear like a unicorn, or escutcheon as decoration. The neck was covered with a crinet on the upper part of the mane, and chain mail over the rest of it. The reins are protected by plates (armored reins) to prevent them from being cut. The breast plate, or peytrel, protected the horse's chest, while the ribs were covered with flanchards, and the hindquarters and with a crupper.

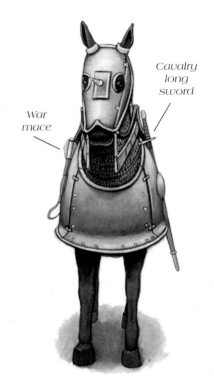

War mace

Cavalry long sword

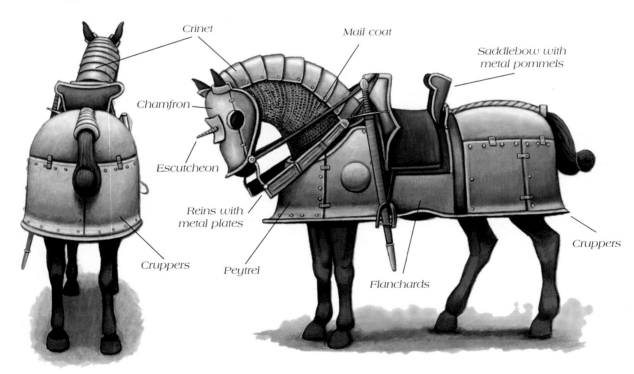

Crinet

Chamfron

Escutcheon

Reins with metal plates

Cruppers

Peytrel

Mail coat

Saddlebow with metal pommels

Cruppers

Flanchards

Views of a horse carrying Gothic armour.

Right: A re-enactor going to a tournament.

throne, initiated the English conquest of the Celtic areas of Wales and Scotland. However, Scotland, led by Robert the Bruce, was a hard nut to crack, and Ireland was not finally subdued until the end of the 16th Century. Edward I had consolidated political and economic power in England, safeguarding a position of power in the throne for its continental aspirants. In 1294, hostilities began against France for the control of Gascony. This lasted until 1297, later to be resumed during the period 1324 to 1327. In 1339 and 1340, confrontations once again occurred between King Philippe IV of France and Edward III of England. After that, there was a series of sporadic and intermittent campaigns of one or two years beginning in 1345 and concluding in 1360. In 1369, the conflict over-flowed into Scotland, Flanders and the Iberian Peninsula.

In 1399, the coronation took place of Henry IV (grandson of the third son of Edward III) after his cousin, Richard II, had been usurped from the throne, thus initiating the rivalry between the houses of Lancaster and York. This eventually led to civil war, known as The War of the Roses, with its attendant upheaval and great bloodshed for 15th Century England.

Throughout these turbulent times, on the continent, the so-called One Hundred Years War was taking place. This began in 1337 and actually lasted for 116 years until 1453, and was between the kingdoms of England and France. This conflict introduced such legendary figures as Joan of Arc and Edward, the Black Prince. The cause of the One Hundred Year War, clearly of a feudal nature, was the purging from French territories of English influence. These territories had been inherited by the English monarch in 1154, when Henry Plantagenet, Count of Anjou, rose to the throne and married Leonore of Aquitaine. The extended conflict finally ended with the English retreating from French territory.

end of Saxon and Scandinavian influence over England. From that point onwards, the Duke of Normandy titled himself 'William the Conqueror' and Norman culture, with a great Frankish input, was yet another to leave it's mark on the island. William reigned in England from 1066 to 1087. Following numerous incidents, Wales and Scotland were, more or less, brought under control, leaving just a few Danish incursions to deal with, although this time they were without the same ferocity of earlier centuries. The Normans gained strategic control of the landscape through the construction of numerous castles, and the introduction of a quite advanced feudal system. Upon his death, William's sons inherited England, as well as the northern part of France (Normandy) paving the way for new disputes in the centuries that followed. Afterwards, three martial kings, Henry II (1154–1189) Richard I the Lionheart (1189-1199) and John I (1199-1216) were the great builders of what was to become England of the 12th and 13th Centuries.

The unfortunate reign of John was plagued by rebellion that was clearly instigated by the nobility, as they continuously pushed for governmental reforms, eventually leading to the signing of the Magna Carta. Later, John's son, Henry III, took a firm military stand over these problems, assisted by his bellicose brother and son. The latter, Edward I, while on the

Norman cavalry during the Battle of Hastings Re-enactment.

HASTINGS
1066

At daybreak on Saturday the 14ᵗʰ October, 1066, Harold's army took the initiative, deploying from an inland position on top of a hill close to Hastings. Meanwhile, William had to approach the position from his fortified coastal bases at Pevensey and Hastings. This allowed the Saxons to control the high ground, always an advantage in any battle. Later, this situation would be a source of sorrow for the Normans. Harold's army, outnumbering the Normans, consisted of around 8000 men. Included among these were almost 800 Housecarls –an elite guard of Danish origin, heavily protected with helmets and mail-coats– and Thegns, wealthy men who could afford a full armour. The remainder of the army was composed of Fyrdmen, peasant militia recruited before the northern battle and numbering about 6500, plus 700 more, recently recruited from adjacent counties. The Norman invasion force numbered around 7500 troops, of which 1500 were archers, 4000 heavy infantry and 2000 cavalry. Harold's army was positioned just on the spur of a hill with a pronounced slope in front, a marshy valley on one flank and a steep embankment on the other. William gave the order to attack, having deployed his force into three divisions. The Bretons on the left wing,

the Normans taking the centre under the king's personal command, and the Franco-Flemish and mercenaries on the right wing. Harold deployed the Housecarls and Thegns with him in the centre, and the Fyrdmen on each wing. The battle began with a rain of arrows falling upon the Saxon infantry, who defended themselves by forming a wall with their interlocked shields. Following this, the Norman left wing mounted a charge, but was repulsed and were then pursued by the Saxon Fyrdmen. William then sent his cavalry behind the Norman rear, riding over the pursuers of the Bretons who had failed with their attack and were broken. At that point, a breach was made in the Fyrdmen right wing that allowed the Normans to attack the Saxon rearguard. William launched his cavalry twice and then he feinted by pretending to retreat. The Saxons set off on pursuit, leaving the safety of the hill position, and breaking up the shield wall. The Normans then turned about and attacked the Saxons who had moved from their natural cover and had dissolved its cohesion. The Saxons broke and fled. King Harold was wounded in the face by an arrow that pierced his brain and he fell and died at the same time as his broken men were in full flight towards the forests.

Norman cavalry during the Battle of Hastings Re-enactment.

Germany

The Eastern Frankish kingdom, that would become modern-day Germany, profited from the dismemberment of the Carolingian empire, as the kings of the Ottonian dynasty managed to overcome the difficulties provoked by the German dukedoms and defeat the Magyars. They even conquered a large swathe of north-western Italy and gained a lot of Slavic territory. The dismemberment of the Empire between Charlemagne's three sons meant the creation of a theoretical, but not an actual empire (Holy Roman Empire) for Louis the Germanic. It was Roman by inherited cultural assimilation, holy by the custom of regarding the figure of the Emperor as sacred by Papal appointment, and Germanic for obvious reasons. As a result of the dismemberment of the Carolingian Empire, a result of the 843 Treaty of Verdun, Louis and his descendants (the last being Louis the Child) would inherit Charlemagne's legacy. After Louis the Child died, Conrad I, a Frank in origin, ruled the Germanic territories for a number of years. Finally,

in 919, the *Reichstag* (a legislative and elective council composed of prominent members of the nobility, church and a delegation of city representatives) chose Henry I, Count of Saxony, to be the king of the Eastern Frankish kingdom. All the Frankish bonds were thus severed, as the new king was of Saxon origin.

It is generally assumed that Otto I, Henry I's son, was crowned emperor of the Holy Roman Germanic Empire in 962. This then became the founding date of the new empire.

One of the military actions that increased the power of the Empire was the definitive defeat of the Magyars at the Battle of Lechfeld in 955. This action halted for good the endemic banditry under which the eastern territories had suffered. The status of Otto I (Otto the Great) was reinforced through his unification policy and his role as the people's defender against the abuses of the feudal nobility.

Otto I's coronation was accepted as an act of transference *(translatio imperii)* from the Roman Empire to the new Empire. That is why the emperors assumed the title of '*Augustus*', which was used during the Late Roman Empire to name two of the four regents in the time of the Tetrarchs. The term '*imperator romanorum*', or emperor of the Romans, was only used after Conrad II attained power. This clearly reveals how much this confederation of Germanic tribes admired the Roman legacy, especially King Henry and his son Otto. Otto I was succeeded by Otto II (973-983), and then by Otto III (983-1002) and, finally, by Henry II (1002-1024). Following the death of Henry II without heir, the Ottonian dynasty became extinct. Following long and heated discussions, Conrad II (1024-1039) was chosen as king by the college of elector princes. Henry III (1046-1056) solved the problems arising between the Frankish and Germanic territories by a determined policy of control over the dukes in the different territories. The title '*Regnum Teutonicum*' was introduced. In 1073, a conflict arose, known as the Investiture Controversy, the origin of which was over the right of the appointing of ecclesiastical posts, by the Pope or by the Emperor. Pope Gregory VII excommunicated King Henry IV (a king since 1056 and an emperor from 1084 to 1106) and this act was to lead to serious consequences. The German nobility elected another king, who was overthrown in 1081 following a war, and the holy institution of the Empire was then subjugated to the Church. The excommunication

Crown, sceptre and other monarchical symbols of the Holy Roman Empire.

was not lifted until after the emperor had paid penance before the Pope at the Castle of Canossa in 1077.

The first member of the House of Hohenstaufen, Conrad III, attained the throne in 1138, thus beginning a new dynasty. The Concordat of Worms was signed in 1122, ending the dispute between the Pope and the Empire, although new disagreements were yet to come.

Frederick I Barbarossa was a monarch of the Hohenstaufen dynasty. He was crowned king in 1152 and assumed the title of emperor between 1155 and 1190. He restored the title of Holy Roman Empire, vindicating the independence of the Empire from the Church and the Holy See.

A recurring phenomenon throughout the 12th Century was the founding of cities, in some cases justified by the population explosion, but in others as a means of increasing the economic power of some strategically placed, fortified towns. Among the cities founded during this century, the most prominent were Munich and Friburg. Frederik Barbarossa was succeeded by his sons Henry VI (1191-1197) and Philip (1198-1208), who was only king of Germany. The next king in line of succession was Otto IV (1209-1215).

Frederick II, the last of the dynasty, was crowned emperor in 1220. He conquered Jerusalem in 1229 during the Sixth Crusade. During Frederick's tenure as emperor of the Holy Empire, he awarded more

Frederick I Barbarrosa

Frederick I Barbarrosa was the son of Frederick II of Swabia and Judith of Bavaria. It is thought that he was born in 1125. He inherited the Swabian dukedom from his father and was elected emperor of the Holy Roman Empire. With his election, the ongoing disputes between the Guelphs (from the House of Welf) and Ghibellines (from the House of Hohenstaufen) came to an end. He pacified the kingdom, limiting the power of the feudal lords, at least at the beginning. He devoted himself to the reawakening of the glory and power of the ancient Roman Empire, focusing his policies on the Italian peninsula. In fact, during one of his military expeditions, he attacked Rome. Pope Adrian IV had no option but to crown Frederick emperor in Rome in July 1154. Frederick Barbarossa became the Pope's ally, and immediately devoted himself to the destruction of the Vatican's enemies. However, the Emperor fell out of favour with the Pope over some misunderstandings and affronts, and was placed under threat of excommunication. In fact, the threat was never carried out as Adrian IV died before fulfilling it. The basic reason behind the constant conflicts between the Holy See and the Empire had to do with the subordination of one institution to the other or vice versa. These disagreements caused the Emperor to fall out with the new Pope, Alexander III. The Pontiff supported the Lombard League, which expelled the imperial troops from Italian territory. In reply to this humiliation, Frederick supported the anti-Pope, Victor III, through whom he could counteract the policies of the Roman Church. The Emperor was excommunicated, but he entered Rome with his armies in 1167 and the Roman Pope was deposed. A new anti-Pope, Pascal III, once again crowned Frederick emperor. The disputes on Italian soil were many, and Frederick suffered a number of setbacks. Eventually Frederik and Alexander

were reconciled and the Peace of Venice signed in 1177, followed by the Peace of Constance in 1183. These treaties confirmed the Emperor's acknowledgement of the Pope's sovereignty over the Papal States, while Alexander acknowledged the Emperor's overlordship over some territories in North Italy and forgive his excommunication. Frederick I Barbarrosa died in 1190, drwoned while crossing the Saleph River in Cilicia, Anatolia (Turkey).

Frederick Barbarossa in a 13th century chronicle.

concessions to the German dukes. His death opened the period known as *Interregnum* that lasted from 1246 until 1273 with the accession of Rudolf I of Habsburg to the throne.

The kings before Henry VII (1312-1313) were merely kings of Germany. It was Henry who reinstituted the title of Emperor of the Holy Empire. After a short reign, he was succeeded by Louis IV (1328-1347), followed by Charles IV (1355-1378), who also assumed the title of emperor.

Economic change throughout the Holy Empire was one of the foremost characteristics of the 13th Century. During this period, the use of money was imposed, even in the rural areas, substituting the bartering and payment in work days. The peasants paid taxes on their lands, thus developing a sense of property that was far from the concepts emanating under feudalism. The 14th Century ended with Wenceslaus (1378-1400) as king of the Romans and Germany, although he was never crowned emperor.

The 15th Century opened with Rupert of Palatinate (1400-1410) who was a very mediocre emperor. During this century, the Holy Empire territories underwent the first conversions that, eventually, would transform them into modern states.

Sigismund of Luxemburg was crowned king in 1410, and he was emperor from 1433 to 1437. He was succeeded by Frederick III, who was crowned king in 1440, and then emperor from 1452 -1493). A mistake made by many of the emperors was to retain their principal residence in their hereditary states, instead of in the traditional territories, the real centers of power. This forced the regents to become involved in many internecine quarrels, thus weakening the Empire. Following a number of conflicts concerning primogeniture among the different pretenders to the Papal throne, a new heresy arose, led by the theologian Jan Hus, that swept the Holy Empire. This was the Hussite heresy, developed in Bohemia and a forerunner of the Protestant reformation.

The Hussites split into two groups: the moderate Ultraquists and the radical Taborites (from the city of Tabor in Southern Bohemia). In 1420, a manifesto known as the Articles of Prague was sent to the king asking for reforms in the liturgy, the cult and other aspects related to the priests and the nobility. By this time, King Sigismund (1410-1437) had died and his brother, Wenceslaus, opposed the reforms proposed by the Hussites and this led to the Hussite Wars of 1419 to 1436. In the beginning, the Taborists held the upper hand but, in 1434, they were eventually subjugated, thanks, in part, to the alliance forged between the Catholics and the Ultraquists. The conflict was solved under the auspices of the Council of Basel, but nothing was the same after the war. Hus became a key contributor to the Protestant movement, the teachings of which had a strong influence on the European states and on Martin Luther himself. During Maximiliam I's reign (1493-1519), the dukes were permitted to call for an Imperial Court in 1495. The formation of this *Reichstag* meant the beginning of the reforms and the subsequent disintegration of the Holy Roman Empire.

Frederick I Barbarrosa in Aachen,
by Albert Bauer.

Following page:
Gothic knights charging enemy infantry.

Lechfeld, 955

The Magyars, a semi-nomadic tribe partially settled in the territories of what is modern-day Hungary, attempted to profit from the Holy Roman Empire's internecine disputes by crossing the Rhine. They had been carrying out constant raids into Eastern Europe throughout the 10th Century, but this time they set out to attack the Western territories. In the beginning, they were allied with a local duke, who had rebelled against his sovereign, but soon disregarded this alliance in order to plunder France. They invaded Bavaria in 955 and put Augsburg under siege with the intention of settling in this capital. For Otto I, this was a good chance to re-establish his authority, which had diminished following the 953-954 rebellion, and to gain a victory. Otto handpicked a number of elite units, including his Saxon Guard, but left the bulk of his army behind. His aim was to make a quick, surprise attack and a large cumbersome army would have spoiled this plan. He also took with him a Bohemian regiment, and troops from the other German dukedoms. It is probably that this force consisted of just between 4000 to 10,000 cavalry forces. The Magyars, meanwhile, outnumbered Otto's small force by about 5-1, and included mounted archers.

Early on the morning of the 10th August 955, as the Imperial army column advanced, following the corridor between the Lech and Schmutter Rivers', the Magyars, profiting from their superior mobility, outflanked the column and attacked its rearguard, driving off the Bohemians in panic, followed shortly later by the Swabians. This should have been the end for Otto's force, but the Magyars stopped and dismounted to loot the German baggage train. This allowed Otto to send the Franks and the Saxon Guard to charge the dismounted units and annihilate them. Otto, with his combined forces, then charged the Magyar line and swept over it, despite a volley of arrows from the Magyar archers that were easily swept aside by the German shields.

Only those Magyars from the elite units offered any solid resistance, as they were equipped with weapons suitable for close combat. However, the bulk of the Magyar army broke and fled, with many of them being killed or wounded in the ensuing pursuit. It is estimated that over 30,000 Magyars were killed, while the remainder were wounded. On their return to Hungary, the surviving Magyar princes were executed and the nomadic thread was broken forever. It was the end of a nightmare. The territories settled by the Magyars were exploited, including Northern Italy, which brought huge benefits to the empire. The Imperial victory was vitally important for the survival of Roman Europe.

Embossed bust of Otto I the Great

Italy

From 493 to 843 A.D., the Italian peninsula was dominated by different waves of Germanic tribes, first the Ostrogoths, later the Lombards and, finally, the Franks. Under the Goth domination, the Italian territories were completely isolated and lived what was to be called a Dark Age. During that period, Lombards, Franks, Byzantines, and, finally, the Germans, invaded the peninsula, destroying everything in their path. In 800, an empire of Frankish origin was created under Charlemagne. He was the selected king of the Lombards, uniting Lombardy with the Empire and was later to be crowned emperor by Pope Leo III. As a consequence, the Vatican States were created and the Pontiff awarded the perpetual title of Roman Patrician to all the French Royal family. The era of invasions ended in 962 when the Holy Roman Empire was created, following the crowning of the German king, Otto I, as emperor by Pope John XII. The lands the Carolingians confiscated from the Lombards were presented to the Pope, who founded the Vatican States in the centre of Italy, which was to become a major political power for centuries. During the 12th Century, competitive and enterprising city states blossomed in Northern Italy, ruled either by the Holy See (Ghibellines) or by the Holy Roman Empire (Guelphs). The Lombard League was an alliance established in 1167 to fight the expansionist policies of the Holy Roman Empire under Frederick I. The League was composed of thirty Northern cities, the main ones being Milan, Bologna, Venice, Cremona, Brescia, Mantua, Bergamo, Padova, Treviso, Verona, Parma and Lodi.

The emperor Frederick I was defeated at the Battle of Legnano (29th May 1176) and he was forced to sign a truce. Thanks to the Treaty of Constanza, the Italian cities recognized imperial sovereignty, providing local jurisdiction was respected.

The League's war against the emperor Frederick II, placed a check on the emperor's expansionist policies in northern Italy.

Panoramic view of Saint Mark's Square in Venice during the Middle Ages.
Anonymous oil on canvas. Venetian School.
Fine Arts and Archeology Museum, Besançon, France.

Bartholomew Colleoni

Colleoni was born in 1400 in the village of Solza, Lombardy. He belonged to a noble family that had left its land due to the violence created by the Guelphs and Ghibellines. The Young Bartholomew Colleoni began his military career in the service of the condottiero Filippo d'Arcello, Lord of Piacenza. Afterwards, he was in the service of Braccio da Montone fighting against Alfonso V. By 1424, he was fighting under the standard of the Neapolitan baron, Jacopo Caldora, against his former lord, da Montone. Colleoni's military knowledge was a key factor during the siege of Bologne in 1425. Later, he devoted himself to the defense of the Republic of Venice, under the command of Francesco Gonzaga. His great prestige and numerous deeds were rewarded by a high position in the Venetian army. In 1434, he was under the command of Erasmus de Narni, the famous Condottiero Gattamelata. Following the signing of the peace accord between Venice and Milan, in 1443 he joined the Milanese under the command of Francesco Sforza. He fought in numerous battles including Verona, Brescia and Lake Garda. He was charged with treason after this last change of side, and was imprisoned. The Milan-based Visconti's never forgave him for passing into Venetian service. He remained in prison until the Duke of Visconti's death in 1447. On his release, he was at the service of Sforza for one year, but then returned to Venetian service, being appointed captain general for life in 1455. It is said that he was one of the most honest and faithful Condottieri of the time, since nobody could ever prove that he had betrayed any Lord or had carried out any criminal plundering, unlike the majority of the soldiers of fortune.

In 1475, following the deaths of his wife and daughter, Bartholomew Colleoni left the eventful life of a Condottiero and retired to the Castle of Malpaga in Bergamo, where he died on the 2nd November that year.

The Republic of Florence was one of the foremost Italian cities due to its economic power, and especially following the annexation of Siena. The Medici family became all-powerful in this city.

The Dukedom of Milan was the largest economic power in northern Italy. In the beginning it was a republic, but later it became a dukedom ruled over by the Visconti family. After the Sforza's deposed the Visconti's, the dukedom was presented to the king of France, Louis XII, a Visconti relation. Later, following the war between Francis I of France and Charles I of Spain, the dukedom passed into Spanish hands

The equestrian statue of Bartholomew Colleoni in St Mark's Square, Venice. Sculpted by Verrochio.

The Longships, Drakkars, and the Viking incursions

Viking longships were designed to be the fastest, most versatile and lightest vessels of their time. They could navigate in water less than a metre deep, and the Vikings were able to row these ships forwards or backwards without turning the ship about. This was a great advantage when escaping after a raid. The average length of a longship was 28 metres and it carried a crew of twenty to thirty oarsmen, who rowed the ship when the winds were slight or calm. Each ship was owned by a nobleman and among the other members of the crew was a helmsman, who steered the ship, and a lookout that watched for rocks in shallow waters. The remaining men onboard were warriors, eager to do battle or to raid, and who took the place of a tired or ill oarsman.

The first recorded attack by the Vikings was in 793, when they razed the Lindisfarne monastery, located off England's northeast coast. On landing, they disembarked very quickly, looted the coastal villages, killing and capturing the inhabitants as slaves. The coastal regions of Germany, France and Great Britain lived under the Viking terror for decades. They were a real nightmare for the western European coastlines, with no one seemingly able to put an end to the raids. By the end of the 9th Century, the Vikings became more adventurous and they undertook an actual invasion of England. They plundered cities, including Hamburg, Utrecht and Rouen. By navigating the Seine, they placed Paris under siege for almost a year without success but escaped with an immense amount of booty. In the Muslim Iberian Peninsula they reached Seville by rowing up the Guadalquivir River, and they raided the Mediterranean coasts. It was not until the end of the 10th Century that the Vikings ceased their raiding due, primarily, to their conversion to Christianity. A number of kingdoms were created in Scandinavia, and their monarchs then devoted themselves to their individual country's development.

why she appointed her grand-nephew, Erik of Pomerania, as her successor. Margaret summoned the chief councillors of the three monarchies to the Swedish city of Kalmar, where Erik was crowned, and the Act of Union, The Kalmar Union, was written in 1397. From then on, the same king ruled the three countries until the Union was revoked in 1523 by Christian II.

Vikings before the battle. Hastings, 2006

Vessels, like this replica longship, opened new trade routes and sailed the oceans to raid other peoples and even discover new lands.

Spain, the Western Crusade

The Iberian Peninsula of the 10th Century had suffered under Islamic expansionism along the western coasts of the Mediterranean. As already mentioned, the Franks, led by Charles Martel, halted the Muslim advance at Poitiers in 732. Along the Eastern borders, the other extreme of Saracen expansionism, Byzantium attempted to hold back the onslaught until the European kingdoms realised that the Muslims were a real threat. This led to a universal call for a Crusade that, in the end, would result in eight bloody expeditions to the Holy Land between 1095-1270. In 1031, the Omeya caliphate, which ruled the territories of peninsular Spain called *Al-Andalus* by the Muslims, was divided into small kingdoms, or *Taifas*. New Berber tribes crossed the Gibraltar Strait and took over from the Arab Omeya dynasty.

The first tribe to do so were, the Almoravides, ruling from 1085 and 1147, followed by the Almohads who were, more or less dominant until 1227.

So, the scene was set for a struggle for supremacy between the two opposing sides, the Christian Hispanic kingdoms, which had emerged at the end of the Visigoth period and the fall of the Roman Empire, and the Taifas kingdoms, united under Islam, yet divided and acting individually. The Christian kingdoms were unified under the influence of the kingdom of Castile and fought with the ultimate vision of a unified Roman Hispania. At first, military operations were focused basically on raids and the subjugation of a number of weak fortified towns. Little-by-little, the Hispanic kingdoms conquered new territories that had then to pay them taxes, progressively weakening them while, at the same time, making the con-

Castle of the Temple at Ponferrada, Leon.

querors ever more wealthy. By this process, the Christian *Reconquista* was seen more as a Crusade, and the new military orders, composed of warrior monks, were key factors in this new vision. In 1128, the Order of the Temple began to undertake military operations on the Peninsula, so too the Order of the Hospitalers or Order of Saint John in 1136. These were followed in 1158 by the Castilian Order of Calatrava and in 1170 the Order of Santiago, or Saint Jacob, the Leonese Order of Alcantara in 1177, and the Order of Montesa from Aragon in 1317. In the territories where the *Reconquista* was being carried out, there were no permanent armies. On the contrary, urban militias, comprised of knights, men-at-arms and peasants, were specially recruited for each battle. So, following each successful battle, the army dispersed so it was impossible to hold the conquered territory. This was the reason the Hispanic kingdoms monarchs had to seek help from well equipped and trained military orders composed of highly motivated, trained soldiers. The Orders built and defended castles in the recently conquered territories. They were a fast intervention force on the borders of the kingdoms. Many of the orders took their names from castles and cities whose defence had been entrusted to them, including Alcantara, Calatrava and Montesa. For example, the knights belonging to the Order of Calatrava were entrusted, by the outstanding king of Castile, Alfonso VIII, with the protection of the Christian advance area to the south of Toledo. In 1174, They were given the rights over every castle captured from the enemy, a fifth part of the ones captured in the future, and a tenth part of the crown's total income. The king of Aragon did the same by giving Alcañiz castle to the same order.

Al-Mansur, also known as Almanzor, one of the foremost Almohad leaders and caliph, led his troops from North Africa to Cordoba in 1190. His mission was to eradicate the kingdom of Castile. The king of Castile, Alfonso VIII, gathered his men at Toledo and deployed them in Alarcos, but they were totally defeated by the Muslims. The castle of Calatrava and other surrounding fortresses were lost and the Muslims advanced northwards. As they did so, in 1196 the Grand Master of the Order of

ALFONSO VIII

Alfonso VIII was born in Soria on 11th November 1155. He was the son of Sancho III and Blanch of Navarre. He became king at the early age of three, following the death of his father. His mother had died giving birth to him. As usually happened in these cases, a dispute emerged, leading to war between two opposing noble factions. On the one side were the Houses of Lara and Castro, fighting for the regency and the tutelage of the child, Alfonso, while, one the other, the same was sought by his uncle, Fernando, king of Leon. In consequence, as an object of dispute, Alfonso had a turbulent childhood. Some thought it better to keep him alive, while others sought to kill him. With his life at risk, a group of Castilian nobles took him safety in Soria and, later, to Avila. On 11th November 1169, Alfonso was knighted at the Monastery of San Zoilo. At the age of fourteen, he became the King of Castile. From the beginning, his primary concern was to recover all the territories lost during the war the nobles had fought during his childhood. He signed an alliance with Alfonso II of Aragon. In 1170, at the age of 15, he married Eleanor Plantagenet, she being a mere nine years old but she was the daughter of the king of England, Edward II, and Eleanor of Aquitaine, sister of Richard I Lionheart. From that date, his aim was the unification of the Hispanic kingdoms and actively promoted new campaigns of conquest or Reconquista. He achieved a crucial victory against the Almohad Empire in 1212 at the Battle of Las Navas de Tolosa, a fact not fully recognised of its importance by modern historians. In addition to his military deeds, Alfonso VIII founded the first Spanish university at Palencia: the Studium Generale. Alfonso died as king of Castile in Avila on 5th October 1214. This glorious, self-sacrificing and humble man was the king who unified Spain in those turbulent years. Castile became, in this way, the main unifying force of the Hispanic kingdoms. The hegemony of Castile is easily understandable, as this kingdom had spilt more blood during the Reconquista and had formed a new nation, as did the English and French kingdoms.

Alfonso VIII
19th century engraving.

Calatrava, Nuño Pérez de Quiñonez, in a daring strategic manoeuvre, instead of going north to confront them, advanced southwards, entered the Moors region and re-conquered the Salvatierra region. Then in 1198, Quiñonez made the castle of Salvatierra his headquarters and the main convent. However, in 1211, the Muslims recaptured it and held it until 1226.

Almanzor, who was victorious at Alarcos thanks to his larger army, was unable to keep his army together as it consisted of North African volunteers, and was forced to sign a truce, which was also very convenient for the Christian king. Once the period of the truce was over, Alfonso resumed military operations. In response, the new caliph, *Al-Nasir*, Prince of the Believers, proclaimed *Jihad* (Holy War) against Christendom and swore to lead his armies to Rome. The caliph gathered his army at Cordoba and advanced towards Salvatierra, laying siege to the fortress of Calatrava. What was considered a strategic loss in the beginning, turned instead into an advantage, as the siege became a time-consuming operation and the propitious campaigning season passed. The Christians, meanwhile, profited from the situation and, in 1212, were able to gather, in the city of Toledo, all the forces willing to defend the Hispanic kingdoms. Just three kings attended this historical meeting: Alfonso VIII, king of Castile; his friend the king of Aragon, Pedro II and, putting aside territorial disputes, the king of Navarre, Sancho VIII. In addition, the military chivalric orders and the Crusaders called by Pope Innocent III also joined the armies of the three kings.

The Christian troops advanced south, re-conquering Malagon and Calatrava. Following this, the French Crusaders deserted due to the paucity of loot they had gathered. On 16th July 1212, *Al-Nasir* was defeated at the Battle of Las Navas de Tolosa, one of Christendom's most significant battles, since the defeat of the three Hispanic kings would have led to the Muslims overrunning the whole of Europe. After the Las Navas de Tolosa battle, the Almohad Empire was convulsed in a severe crisis, with revolts and the resurgence of local warlords. The main Almohad fortresses were

The surrender of Grenada
Detail from the painting by Francisco Pradilla
Ortiz located in the Spanish Senate (1925)

captured by the Christians: Caceres, Merida, Badajoz, Baeza, Seville, and, eventually, Cordoba, the magnificent Omeya caliphate capital city, in 1236. From that moment, the different phases of the *Reconquista* were aimed at the recovery of the Peninsula's eastern territories, by applying pressure on the Murcian taifa and besieging the Grenadan emirate. The foremost supporter of this was the king of Castile, Fernando III, aided by another prominent monarch, the king of Aragon, James I. The king of Aragon had managed to unite the Catalan counties, the kingdoms of Valencia and Majorca under the sovereignty of the Crown of Aragon.

The conquest of the new territories was slowed down by a number of local conflicts in the kingdom of Castile. Following the death of Enrique IV in 1474, the Castilian nobility split into two groups: those in favour of Juana, Enrique's daughter, who was also supported by Portugal, and those in favour of Isabel, the sister of the deceased king and wife of Prince Fernando of Aragon. The schism led to a war with Portugal that was won by Fernando of Aragon, making Isabel the Queen of Castile in 1479. Fernando became the king of Aragon after his father's death. Fernando, a prominent military and political figure of his time, inspired Machiavelli to write 'The Prince'. The couple, Isabel and Fernando, became known as the Catholic Kings and their famous motto was *'Tanto monta monta tanto Isabel como Fernando'*. The spirit of the Crusade was revived with the accession of the Catholic Kings, and every effort was devoted to the expulsion of the Muslims from the Iberian Peninsula. The Nazari emirate, or kingdom of Grenada, came under immense pressure due to the meticulously planned campaigns led by the Christians, while, at the same time, Fernando carried out some very clever diplomatic moves. In April 1491, the Catholic Kings laid siege to Grenada, which fell in January 1492. On 2nd January 1492, Boabdil 'El Chico' surrendered the city's keys to Isabel and Fernando. The Muslim king was sent into exile to a small estate in Las Alpujarras. The last Muslim kingdom in the Peninsula had been defeated.

Boabdil the Moor's last sigh.
Painting by Francisco Pradilla Ortiz (1892)

The Battle of Las Navas de Tolosa
16th July 1212

Once the Christian army had assembled on the battlefield of Las Navas de Tolosa, the Christians totalled 26,950 men, 18,000 from Castile (3000 cavalry and 15,000 infantry), 8500 from Aragon (1500 cavalry and 7000 infantry), and Navarre contributing just 200 knights. There were also around 250 Crusaders who had not deserted, including 150 foreigners, and some Portuguese and Leonese knights who attended of their own volition. In total there were 4950 cavalry and 22,000 infantrymen.

Opposing them was a Muslim army of 51,500 men (6500 cavalry and 45,000 infantrymen), 18,500 were Andalusians with 33,000 Almohads. The Christians deployed in three consecutive lines, each with a central force and two wings on the flanks. The first line, the strongest, with the centre commanded by Diego Lopez de Haro, had an Aragonese wing, under Garcia Romero, on one side, with a Navarre wing on the other. This second one was commanded by Gonzalo Nuñez de Lara, with knights from the Military Orders in the middle and, on the front line, Navarrese and Aragonese wings.

The three kings, escorted by their royal guards, were in the third line. Alfonso VIII in the centre, Sancho VIII of Navarre on the right, and Pedro II of Aragon on the left. Al–Nasir's forces formed up into two lines, also with wings on the flanks, Andalusian volunteers at the front and Almohads behind. This second line had infantry in the centre and cavalry on the flanks. The battle began with a charge by the first line of Christians. The Muslims checked this assault, and the Christian cavalry had to wait for infantry support. The second Christian line was then sent to support its comrades and entered into the melee. The cavalry found itself stationary on the battlefield's ground and the initial inertia was lost. Seeing how desperate the situation had become, with the loss of dynamism and the battle's initiative, Alfonso addressed his two fellow kings, pronouncing, 'Here we are to die!' and charged against the Muslim mass, inspiring the others to follow him. This third charge, led by the three kings, was crucial for the ensuing victory. The Moorish army, along with their caliph, fled the field.

The Battle of Las Navas de Tolosa.
Oil on canvas by Francisco de Paula Van Halen. Spanish Senate. Madrid.

Holy War in the East
The Crusades

While, in the West, most of the kingdoms were involved in domestic disputes (except the Hispanic kingdoms that were already fighting their own Crusade and, therefore, were acutely aware of the problem) the Middle Eastern Islamic armies continued their religious and territorial expansion. Only the Popes were aware of the danger, especially during the Papacies of Popes Leo IX and Gregory VII. They both realized how the interests of Europe would come under threat by the different Muslim tribes. The outrages committed by the Seleucid Turks threatened not only the pilgrims to the Holy Land and the independence of the Byzantine kingdom, but all of Christendom. Jerusalem was captured in 1070. Although separated from the Catholic Church based on Rome, the emperors of Constantinople asked for help from the Popes. Letters concerning this were exchanged in 1073 between the Byzantine Emperor and Miguel VII and Pope Gregory VII. It was Pope Urban II who followed Gregory VII's plans. A letter from the Emperor of Byzantium, Alexius I Comnenus, to Robert, Earl of Flanders, appeared to be a call for a Crusade, but, in fact, it was merely a request to recruit 500 Flemish knights to reinforce the Imperial army. The Turks, with Antioch falling in 1084, looted Asia Minor and the whole of Syria. In fact, in 1092, the Christians could hold none of the leading Asian metropolises. In 1095, Pope Urban II, the true promoter of the Crusade, under the cry 'Deus vult!' (God wills it), invited the Christian knights to place their swords in the service of God to defend the pilgrims and the Holy places. This exhortation attracted, among others, a deceitful monk called Peter the Hermit, who attracted large crowds of peasants and beggars to the cause. This came to be known as 'the People's Crusade' and it ended in chaos and massacre by the Turks.

FIRST CRUSADE (1069-1099)
Jerusalem is relieved!
The most courageous Frankish, German, Italo-Norman knights joined the Crusade the moment it was launched by the Pope. Among these knights were included the likes of Raymond of Toulouse, Godfrey of Bouillon, Robert of Flanders, Baldwin of Boulogne, Tancred of Hauteville and Bohemond of Taranto. The command of the expeditionary army was given to Raymond of Toulouse, the group's most experienced military commander and who knew the Muslim fighting methods, as he had fought them on the Iberian Peninsula. The Crusader army consisted of 7000 knights and 80,000 infantrymen. The contingent marched to Byzantium, ransacking everything in its path. The agreement signed with the Byzantine Emperor, Alexius, was that the Crusaders would return the re-conquered cities back to Imperial sovereignty and, in exchange, they would get the required logistical support. This happened in the case of the city of Nicaea, but after crossing the Anatolian Peninsula and conquering Antioch, Bohemond disregarded the agreement and proclaimed himself prince. In June 1099, Jerusalem was freed from Muslim control, but only after a long, drawn-out bloody

Godfrey elected as King of Jerusalem.
Oil on canvas by Madrazo & Kuntz
National Museum. Versailles. France

battle with the total number of casualties from both sides estimated at around 80,000. Godfrey was appointed Protector of the Holy Sepulchre. In August of the same year, the Muslims counterattacked but were defeated at Ascalon. Godfrey died in 1100 and was succeeded by his brother, Baldwin, who proclaimed himself King of Jerusalem. By this means, the different Latin kingdoms of the East, the Princedom of Antioch and the Counties of Tripoli and Edessa were formed. Many Europeans remained as settlers and a number of chivalric military orders were founded in the Holy Land, including the Templers, which was devoted to the defence of the Holy Places.

SECOND CRUSADE (1145-1149)

First failure

In the Latin States, the stability achieved following the First Crusade last just fifty years. In 1144, the Turks captured the fortified city of Edessa, thus making the situation unsustainable. This strategic enclave, between the Tigris and Euphrates, was the northern entrance for the Seleucid enemy. Apart from that, the city was where the holy shroud had been discovered, making the loss of the city even more traumatic because of its religious symbolism. However, the Christians profited from this symbolism as it made the propaganda for the launch of a second Crusade more effective. The Pope, Eugene III, ordered the Cistercian monk, Bernard of Clairvaux, to launch a second Crusade. The German and French kings, Conrad III and Louis VII, led the Second Crusade, the primary objective being the retaking of Edessa, and the second being the conquest of Damascus with a more commercial rather than religious intent. The armies of the two kings were set in motion, following the same route as the former Crusade. While crossing Byzantine territory, the emperor, Manuel Comneno, who was still resentful of what had occurred during the First Crusade, refused to aid the Christian armies and devoted himself to intriguing with both Christians and Muslims in search of personal gain. After suffering numerous casualties, due to sustained attacks by the Turks during the march, the force finally reached Syria. The Crusaders then changed their minds and decided to attack the wealthier

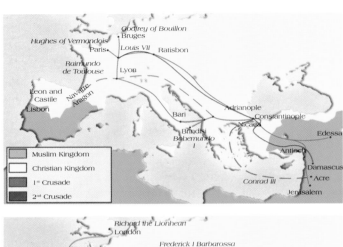

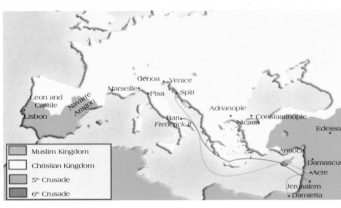

Eight Crusades were launched, but only the first achieved its objective: the liberation of Jerusalem. The other seven were support expeditions to delay the inevitable loss of the Holy sites.

Damascus instead of the symbolic Edessa. The Crusaders conceived a good plan, but the continuous squabbles between the two Christian commanders, who seemed to think they were at a tournament instead of at war, led to a catastrophe. In July 1148, Damascus was placed under siege, but when the Crusaders received news of the advance of a Muslim army, they raised the siege and deployed for a pitched battle. Finally, a year later, the Crusaders were forced to retreat home with heads hung low.

THIRD CRUSADE (1189-1192)
Jerusalem has fallen!

The most prominent character during the Third Crusade was the Kurd, *Salah ad Din Yusuf ibn Ayyub*, better known as Saladin. He was a great leader, a lover of literature and culture in general, intelligent and a gifted strategist. He was also both brave and compassionate for the defeated. He was born in 1137 to a noble Ottoman family. He ruled wisely and his influence stretched over a vast empire stretching from Tripoli to the Tigris River and from Armenia to the Indian Ocean. He introduced Sunni thought into Egypt, when the Fatimi caliphate collapsed in 1171 and he seized power, and founded the Ayyubi dynasty. After the death, in 1174, of the Sultan who had sent him to Egypt, Saladin devoted himself to the conquest of Syria, capturing Damascus, Mosul and Aleppo. He advanced towards the Latin States, capturing Acre and other strong cities. Ben Saladino Sultan he defeated the Christian king, Guido, at the Battle of Hattin in 1187, a victory that opened the gates of Jerusalem. The Third Crusade was launched to recover Jerusalem. Two kings and an emperor joined the expedition: Richard I Lionheart of England, Philippe II August of France and Frederick I Barbarossa. The French and English sailed to the Holy Land, as they considered this the safer option. The Germans, however, travelled overland, but Frederick was tragically drowned in a river in Anatolia before reaching his objective and the German army broke up. Following this, the French and English contingents, after spending the winter of 1190 at Messina, Sicily,

Louis VII of France at Saint-Denis, 1147.
Oil on canvas by Jean Baptiste Mauzaisse.
National Museum, Versailles, France

Godfrey of Bouillon

(1061-1100)

Godfrey was born in Baisy (modern Belgium) in 1061 into a noble family. His father was the Count of Boulogne, who claimed descent from Charlemagne. When his uncle died, Godfrey received the County of Verdun and the Mark of Anvers. He later received the title of Duke of the Low Lorraine (Low Countries) from the emperor of the Holy Empire, Henry IV. He retained a good relationship with the emperor who, in return, received Godfrey's assistance on a number of different military expeditions within the Empire, and even one against the former Pope. After selling the great part of his domains, he departed for the Holy Land with a large, powerful Flemish and Walloon army. He was 34 years old when he began the venture. He was the typical medieval hero, possessing an impressive physical appearance and a rational, restrained character. Although the theoretical leader of the Crusade was Raymond of Toulouse, following his victories at Nicaea, Doryleaum and Antioch, Godfrey became the actual moral leader of the expedition. In 1099, after a terrible siege, Jerusalem fell and he was elected by his own men 'King of Jerusalem', a title he rejected with the famous sentence: 'Nobody will wear a golden crown in the same place where Christ wore the crown of thorns'. However, he did accept the title of 'Defender of the Holy Sepulchre'. The new Latin Kingdom of Jerusalem was established. It included modern Israel, the south of the Lebanon and some territories in Jordan and Syria. In August 1099, an army advanced from Egypt towards Jerusalem to liberate it from the Franks (a term used by the Muslims when referring to the Crusaders). Godfrey and his men waylaid the Muslims at Ascalon, with Christians triumphant in the ensuing battle, and the Holy Land was pacified for many years.

On 18th July 1100, the energetic Godfrey succumbed to a strange illness and died. It is believed that he was poisoned by the Saracens with a meal during the course of peace negotiations.

resumed the expedition and took the island of Cyprus, thanks in part to the reinforcements that had been sent from England in 1191. During the summer, the two fleets disembarked at Acre, which had been under siege for two years by the Crusaders of the free Latin States. On 12th July 1191, Acre surrendered and the monarchs were under the impression that it was their presence that had forced the capitulation. They shared the loot and the French king, considering his mission completed, decided to return home with his army. Only the English army and the Crusaders gathered by the former King of Jerusalem, Guido de Lusignac, remained in the Holy Land. Richard the Lionheart accepted the challenge and defeated Saladin on 7th September 1191. The Treaty of Jaffa was signed under which the Muslims compromised by allowing the pilgrims to enter the Holy City, even though it was still under their rule. Richard, meanwhile, was in a hurry to return home to England to sort out his domestic problems caused by his brother John.

FOURTH CRUSADE (1202-1204)
The Sacking of Constantinople

In 1198, Pope Innocent III launched a new Crusade to recover Jerusalem. It was preached by the Frenchman, Fulk of Neuilly, and commanded by the Italian noble, Boniface of Montferrat. On this occasion, the Crusade was not led by kings, but by nobles in search of glory and wealth. During the summer of 1202, the new Crusaders departed for the East. However, on reaching Venice to board the transports, the ambitious *Dux* demanded full payment of the huge transport fee. To enable them to meet the cost, the Crusaders were forced to conquer the Dalmatian city of Zara, belonging to the king of Hungary, and use the looted wealth as a payment for the crossing. This was a Crusade of plunder from the very beginning. The Crusaders looted wherever they went and they became extremely greedy. Their next objective was the weak Byzantine capital, Constantinople. At the time, the city

Godfrey takes Jerusalem, July 14, 1099.
Engraving, Library of Catalonia, Barcelona, Spain.

was immersed in a domestic dispute and was easy prey. The Crusaders sacked the city and placed on the throne the overthrown Isaac II. Constantinople was sacked once again in 1204, and the government shared between the Crusaders and the Venetian patriarchs, who profited vastly from the situation as they could control the Dardanelles sea passage from the Black Sea, thus favouring their own commercial interests.

FIFTH AND SIXTH CRUSADES
1217-1221 and 1229-1243

The Fifth Crusade was also launched by Pope Innocent III, and was supported and jointly led by Leopold VI of Austria and Andrew II of Hungary. The troops began their march in August 1217. It had the same objective as the Fourth Crusade, namely striking at the heart of the Ayyubid dominions in Egypt. They first occupied the port of Damietta, at the mouth of the Nile, which protected the entrance to the Latin States, and then turned their attention on Cairo. In the summer of 1221, they established a camp fortress by the Nile, but the sultan, Al-Kamil, ordered the opening of the dikes during the flooding season and the camp was left surrounded by marshes. The result was a debacle and the Crusaders had to abandon even the conquered territory, including Damietta.

The organization of the Sixth Crusade was somewhat atypical. The Pope had imposed a penance on the Emperor of the Holy Roman Empire, Frederick II Hohenstaufen, which could only be expiated by going on a Crusade. The emperor accepted the penance, but he delayed the preparations for the expedition. This gave Pope Gregory IX the excuse to excommunicate him. Finally, Frederick II, who had dreamt all his life of becoming King of Jerusalem, decided to ignore the Pope and departed for Holy Land in 1228. Surprisingly, Frederick became the master of Jerusalem through diplomatic means and the weakness of the Ayyubid, who were involved in internal disputes and had no wish to fight the

Pope Urban II preaches the First Crusade at the Council of Clermont.
Illustration from the Chronicle of William of Tyre, 13th Century.
Public and University Library of Geneva, Switzerland.

Pope Urban II
(1042-1099)

His birth name was Odon and he was born in Lagery, near Châtillon-sur-Marne, France, in 1042. He, too, came from a noble family. He studied at Reims and later was sent to the Monastery of Cluny, the real intellectual see of the Catholic Church. He became the prior of the Monastery in 1073. In 1079, with the support of Pope Gregory VII, he was appointed Cardinal Bishop of Ostia and, in 1084, sent to Germany. In 1088, he was elevated to the Holy See by succeeding Gregory VII and becoming Supreme Pontiff, taking the name Urban II. The first years of his pontificate were fraught with difficulty, as he had to deal with the so-called 'Dispute of the Investitures' and the anti-pope, Clement III, who had been appointed by the emperor of the Holy Roman Empire Henry IV, who was excommunicated. Henry was not to be the only king excommunicated by Urban II. The king of France, Philippe I, received the same sanction for repudiating his wife. Urban II was an active and polemic man who was involved in political affairs, and who acted with more skill than his predecessor. He revealed himself as a real diplomat by negotiating the schism between Byzantium and the Roman Church. Urban II knew all too well what was going on in the Islamic world and he was convinced that it would be a tough competitor for Christianity. Urban was aware of the fragmentation of the Abassi caliphate of the Fatimites (Muslims of the Shia branch), who suffered under the raids of the Seleucid Turks and who eventually captured Jerusalem and Syria. The Seleucid were Sunni Muslims who were extremely intolerant of other religions. These geostrategic changes in the Middle East forced Urban II to launch the First Crusade in 1095. After finally ridding himself of the anti-Pope, Clement III, Urban died in 1099 before receiving the news of the liberation of Jerusalem.

Christians for a single city. Frederick proclaimed himself King of Jerusalem in 1229, after gaining Bethlehem and Nazareth among others.

SEVENTH AND EIGHTH CRUSADES
1248-1250 and 1250-1270

In 1244, the Muslims undertook another successful campaign against the Christian territories, and Jerusalem was lost yet again. In answer, the devout king of France, Louis IX (Saint Louis), launched the Seventh Crusade, but it was received with little enthusiasm despite Pope Innocent IV preaching the Crusade in 1245. Louis' Christian army advanced on Damietta in 1250, where it was defeated. The King of France was captured in Mansura, Egypt, along with all his troops. After spending four years in the Holy Land, paying a ransom for his freedom and returning Damietta, the king returned to France where he devoted himself to the construction of different

fortresses. Aware of the enormous strength of the Mongol Empire, the Christians tried to entice them to their cause by converting them to Christianity. In the end, the alliance between the two civilizations became unworkable, as the fierce, belligerent Mongols had other aims in mind. In 1268, the strategic city of Antioch was lost. Across Europe, this news was received with great trepidation and a new Crusade was launched as an immediate response. Back in France, Louis IX supported the Eighth Crusade of 1269 with the stated aim of conquering Tunisia to make it a buffer state to protect Europe from the Muslim threat. However, the real reason was somewhat different: Charles of Anjou, king of Naples, Louis' brother, wanted to eliminate the competition from the Tunisian traders. Whatever the reasoning behind the venture, while in Tunisia, Louis and the majority of his men succumbed to the Black Death. And so, in 1270, crusading came to an ignominious conclusion.

A wonderful view of Constantinople from the Galata Bridge.
Painting by Hermann David Soloman

EUROPE IN 13ᵀᴴ CENTURY

FINLAND

Uppsala

Reval •

LIVONIA

• Novgorod

• Visby

Riga •

Baltic Sea

SAMOGITIA

TERRITORY OF NOVGOROD

• Königsberg

• Marienburg

RUSSIAN PRINCIPALITIES

• Tannenberg

iezno

POLAND   Lublin •

• Kiev

• Cracow

Caspian
Sea

a • • Pest

KINGDOM OF
HUNGARY

• Belgrade

KINGDOM OF
SERBIA

Black Sea

Ragusa

Adrianople •

• Durrës

Constantinople

SELJUKS

Brindisi

Thessalonika •

LATIN
EMPIRE

• Nicaea

• Dorylaeum

• Caesarea

• Sardis

• Edessa

• Laodicea

• Antioch

Athens •

• Atalia

Candia •

KINGDOM OF
CYPRUS

• Emesa/Homs

• Tripoli

CRETE

• Damascus

KINGDOM
OF
JERUSALEM

ARABIA

Jerusalem •

• Damietta

• Ashkelon

Alexandria

MEDIEVAL TOURNAMENTS

The Birth of Simulated War

The birth of tournaments, or what can be called simulated war, had its origins in the exercises practised by the ancient Romans. These *hippica gymnasia* consisted of mock combat between two cavalry teams who threw blunt javelins at each other while, at the same time, circling their opponents. This exercise was called the 'Cantabrian charge or circle', which loosely translates into attacking an opponent while simultaneously moving around him. This, then, is the origins of the word 'tournament', or 'turning around' something in a simulated battle.

According to a 12th Century chronicler Godofredo Malatesta, a Norman Sicilian knight, called Galfridus of Pruliaco, already held tournaments on the island of Sicily in 1000. A later chronicle, based on the mythical Arthurian legends by Geoffrey of Monmouth or Chetrien of Troyes, tells of the celebration of a tournament at the court of Camelot by the legendary King Arthur in 1100. Some years later, the famous English knight, champion of many tournaments,

Lithography displaying a medieval joust between two knights.

of his education as a future knight. A squire was a young noble, and he was obligated to observe a number of rules of conduct associated with the nobility, such as the defence of honour, the sanctity of oaths and of the given word, fraternity among its members, and being able to perform well in activities related to weapons practice, such as hunting, war, jousts and tournaments. Other concepts such as fame, honour, loyalty and service were ideals that shaped a positive, archetypal image of the nobility. The squires' duties included the cleaning of weapons and armour, assisting the knight to dress, taking care of his equipment and belongings and even guarding his master's dream. Squires assisted a knight by carrying his weapons and holding his horses, tending to his wounds, removing him from the battlefield or the tournament field if wounded,

and, finally, being in charge of the burial of his master if he fell.

In tournaments, jousts and battles the squires were to assist their master in all his requirements. They even fought side-by-side with their knights. A knight avoided fighting the squires, preferring to fight other knights. On the other hand, squires always wanted to fight a knight to achieve a higher standing. Any squire distinguishing himself during the course of a pitched battle could gain the recognition of a lord and be knighted on the battlefield.

The training of a squire included all kind of lessons, such as reading, writing, music, performing games, dancing and singing. At the age of 21, a young, educated squire could be promoted to the rank of knight. After being ordained, the young knight had to observe a number of rules relating to his daily behaviour. Personal

*Medieval Tournament.
Miniature from the 'Grandes
Chroniques de France'.
Castle of Chantilly, France.*

lack of basic rights. Two examples of such women who managed to stand out, thanks to their noble origin and, therefore, access to education, were Eleanor of Aquitaine, Queen of France and then of England, and Isabel the Catholic, Queen of Castile. Eleanor represents the harmony between beauty and intelligence, something so sought after by modern women. The role of the ladies in the tournament was a reference to the medieval literature of the epic poems in which the knight can show off his skills as a warrior, at the Court close to his lady, unlike on a battlefield. The tournament was, therefore, a conjunction of interests between the masculine desire to show off and courtesan wooing. Knights took it upon themselves to defend the honour and life of their sweethearts, and these warriors carried a garment, cloth or other keepsake belonging to the chosen one that justified all their efforts during the battles.

Another important figure in the tournaments was the herald. They were the chief referees, and they decided on controversial situations, their decision not being open to appeal. All of them were members of the highest families. Some of them had been former champions, and they dictated the rules in this sport and military events. They knew the origins and merits of all those who hoped to join a fight reserved for the knights belonging to the noblest origin.

The coat of arms was the knight's identity card. His courage, loyalty and bravery were reflected on it. It also represented the history of his family, the honour and the good name he had to defend at all costs and which had been gained thanks to a battle or tournament.

In fact, the heralds were in charge of the records of all kinds of deeds. They were influential persons who decided who deserved to join a tournament. Their duties included knowing the origin of heraldry as a science that researched and recorded, through the medium of the coats of arms, the quality of the different houses of nobility of a realm.

image was extremely important. A noble knight had to quiet spoken, moderate with food and alcoholic drinks, and able to take care of his dress. Exterior appearance defined the differences between the different social groups and they were a distinction of rank. Inappropriate conduct, such as dice gambling or betting on weapons and horses were unacceptable according to the ideals of Chivalry, especially those displayed during a campaign.

The ladies of the medieval world represented the exaltation of the feminine virtues, although they were not recognized at all by law or rights. Some noble women attained prominence despite their

Good race
A Pre-Raphaelite painting by Edmund Blair Leighton.

Two re-enactors performing as mounted king of arms and a herald.

and 1271, until it was besieged and captured by the Mameluke Sultan Beibars on the April 8th 1271, after he had tricked the Hospitallers.

Siege Weapons
Medieval Poliorcetics

Holding a castle in siege was always a difficult, costly operation. The assailant had to deploy a force much larger than the garrison defending the fortress. None of the besiegers would know how many archers, crossbowmen, lancers or knights comprised the garrison, or even if an army had taken refuge. A clear example of this is offered by the Krak des Chevaliers, known by the Arabs as the mountain, an impregnable redoubt with a permanent garrison of 2000 men, with the possibility of accommodating a further 1000. The Krak des Chevaliers consists of two concentric lines of defence and an outer curtained wall with several cylindrical towers. This construction is extremely solid, created for a deep defence of the territories dominated by it. This castle was formed by concentric rings of walls to prevent a surprise attack, keeping the shooting range of the enemy's siege weapons far from the heart of the castle. Its walls are made of stone ashlars measuring 35cms high and 1m long. On one occasion, Saladin rode out to inspect the defences of this mighty castle before attacking it. He retired without even attempting a single assault.

Because of this, it is easy to conclude that any assailant would prefer an indirect method for capturing a fortress. A combination of intelligence, diplomacy, negotiation, tricks, psychology, threats and reprisals was required to effect such an outcome. Only when these methods failed, was it deemed necessary to take direct action and siege warfare and poliorcetics knowledge were applied.

The Krak des Chevaliers in Syria.

THE CASTLE AND ITS ROOMS

FOOT SOLDIERS' LIVING QUARTERS

STABLES

CHAPEL

GUARDHOUSE

DRY MOAT